Africa and Her Children

To Hakim,   6/19/83

I hope you read this book and
then tell me about it

                    H. Amon

Africa
and Her Children

An Introduction to the Origin of Civilization

HARRY ARMORER

Exposition Press   *Hicksville, New York*

Contents

Preface

I wrote this book to inform the world of the wisdom of the African forefathers and the continuing contribution of Africa's children. Much sacrifice—primarily in terms of money and time—has been made to produce this book; prior to this encounter, I never gave thought to the necessities of such a production. The endless hours of reading, writing, and rewriting did not become apparent to me until I was involved in the experience myself. I feel that the information in the book has made the total effort worthwhile and rewarding, and I hope that you will agree with me after you have read the book.

I started African studies in the early fifties with Cyril Murray—an able and knowledgeable historian and teacher, who motivated me to write, not by his words but by his deeds. I made several attempts to write, but not until September 1960 did I really begin. However, I gave up after a few months, realizing that I did not have enough time to devote to the task. In addition, I needed to do more research. During this period, I got more involved with J. A. Rogers's works on the history of Africa and her children. His classical contributions sent me scurrying in several directions to libraries, bookstores, museums, and so forth. During one of these visits I met Richard B. Moore at his bookstore, which was called The Frederick Douglass Bookstore. I came to know him well and worked with him through his committee in selling his book, *The Name Negro and Its Origin and Evil Use.*

As a matter of course, I attended lectures, meetings, and symposia that really broadened my scope, and the shocking knowledge I received of the greatest contributions of the world aided in my motivation, which I had as a youngster, to write this book. In 1967, I seriously began to write and have been at it ever since.

The book is written about Africa and her children, but is for all people of the world to read, for Africa's history is the world's way of life and therefore touches everyone. I have tried to write in such a manner that makes for easy reading and, at the same time, have tried to be informative and comprehensive. If at times it seems as though I am overemphasizing a fact or am being repetitious, bear with me—I believe my words are necessary, and I feel that when you are partway through the book you will agree with me.

History is defined as the ability of a person to give a systematic account of persons, places, and things. This is what I have set out to do, and I hope I have fulfilled my goal.

I must mention here that I could not have accomplished this book without the assistance, consideration, and sacrifice of my wife, Audra, and my children, Gail, Ayshia, Makeda, and Sharifa. Gail edited and Ayshia read, rewrote, and typed my manuscripts; Makeda "manned" the dictionary, and Sharifa continually encouraged me. I hope that my presentation is enlightening enough to motivate the world to visualize Africa and the contributions of her children.

Africa and Her Children

1

In Search
of the African Forefathers

The main purpose of this book is to alert those of us who did not have the opportunity to study about our ancestors to the history of our past. Its aim is to tell the truth regardless of where it may lead us. This book may leave the reader with some questions or doubts about the information it provides, or it may cause him to seek more information elsewhere. Whichever it may do for you, it would be a great accomplishment, because as long as you are stirred into motion, you are sure to become emotionally involved in the most important subject of the universe: THE ORIGIN OF THE ORIGINAL PEOPLE OF THE UNIVERSE AND THEIR GREAT CONTRIBUTIONS.

Every person has a beginning which is the foundation for their culture and pride, and which enhances dignity and results in the determination to achieve, accomplish, and challenge the future.

Have you ever noticed the pride and dignity that different nationality groups show in their parades, marches, private organizations, et cetera? Again, all this motivates a person to progress. I would like you to study the material carefully and then give serious thought to the historical facts, for, as we start from the beginning and proceed to the present, the thoughts and stigmas that many people have about the African ancestors will change into pride and dignity. We can, together, learn of all

1

the contributions that Africa and the African fathers have made to the world—contributions that are still being used today.

Blacks must know who they are, and they can't know who they are without first learning of their past, which is the history of Africa and Africans. I will attempt to do this shortly, and, as we proceed with this and other chapters, maybe you can add some more facts. With each passing day, more and more facts are being discovered, and, as the trend of history demonstrates, each of these facts probes further into African antiquity. In this chapter, I will discuss the study of man. If you learn nothing other than the value of pride and dignity, you will have learned much.

In the beginning, there was darkness and no life, and God decided to brighten the earth. He said, "Let there be light," and there was; and, as the Bible tells us, God created living things: men, animals, birds, fishes, trees, and so forth. We are now at the beginning of life.

Whatever culture we have today has developed from the artifacts of yesterday, and this culture is the steppingstone to tomorrow. Every implement, machine, or other device of today is derived from a previous idea; and, as insignificant as it may seem, the most important aspect of any culture is the conception of an idea and the subsequent utilization of that idea for personal and recipient benefits.

Man's use of nature probably began when he chipped the first flint or broke the first branch of a tree to make a tool or weapon. Such an action was an original idea which led to the improvisions that caused man to evolve to higher and higher planes.

It seems that the aforementioned primitive discoveries and inventions are what made people come together in the formation of tribes or societies, which were so instrumental in forming a civilization.

To review what was just said, let us consider the following. When the first rock was used, the derived utilizations initiated man's hunting activity, which in turn required that he roam away from home. This resulted in the triggering of many other ideas and discoveries. The rock was used to cut tree branches or for picking fruits and flowers from the tree. Also, the rock was used to make shelters or even as a defense against wild animals and from other men. Through this multiplicity of ideas and discoveries, man was forced to talk and thus widen his scope of communication.

When men were forced to live together, by the very nature of their discoveries, they formed a culture—a group that fished, hunted, traded, ate, and slept together. The activities created this culture, which again caused a multiplicity of other material things to happen, for necessity is the mother of invention and creation. Taking these things into consideration and trying to visualize life at that time, we notice that man was not totally occupied. He had much time to think, discover, and form ideas, which greatly led to the improvement of his environment.

Scientists have given the stages of man and certain periods names; I will, however, try to avoid, as much as possible, all the scientific names and instead use more relative descriptions, so that this history will not become boring. It is well known that the study of history has a tendency to become bogged down in terminology, not to mention the very dry style of the writing—which oftentimes seems directed at an audience of professors. However, let us resume our course through history.

Men necessarily grouped together in tribes, villages, and so forth. It became a necessity to invent and then modify their inventions, so as to be able to cope with a more sophisticated society. For example, man fished from the banks and, in so doing, chased the fish away. Eventually, man made boats and later developed traps, nets, and other means of snaring fish.

As man encountered injury, he had to experiment with healing his wounds. He used mud, sand, and then herbs and powders, and this resulted in medicine—initially dispensed by the medicine man. I state all these things to keep my readers in an alert state of mind, so that later on they can fill in much that I may have missed. In so doing, they will be taking part in the study of man's origin.

Think of the man who built the first shelter—what was that

shelter like? It probably had a roof and a crawlway for an entrance. Next, think of the environmental pressures that would cause man to modify his dwelling. No man would enjoy exposure to the rain or the sun, and neither would he wish to be vulnerable to wild animals and other enemies.

The better the shelter, the better the protection; therefore, man improved his habitat through necessity and not through an urge to be more comfortable. However, many of our modern-day comforts have been derived from the discoveries of common tools, simple machines, and, most of all, common sense. When I said that I wished to keep my readers alert to fill in some of the points I may have missed, my intention was that they use their imagination; for instance, what did the hunter do with the fish after he had snared it?

The first man on earth, the original man, the African, the Black man, was the beginning of human life. The Bible, one of our oldest history books, tells us so; but as it is common among people to doubt history, especially the foremost issue of the origin of the human race, more recent information will be used to make this point. Prominent scientists, anthropologists, and historians within the grasp of present memory have found the oldest human bones and other artifacts in Africa; but to be specific, the oldest human remains were found in Kenya and Tanganyika in the heart of Africa. They date as far back as 2.5 million years. At this point, my analysis of the past may not stir your emotions, but as we proceed along and learn of things more relevant to our lives, we will become more cognizant of Africa's glorious past. Just think for a minute now . . . for anything to evolve there must be a beginning, and the Black man was that beginning, and he proceeded on to advance to various civilizations. These civilizations will be discussed later, as will the identity of the original man—the Black man, the African.

Archeologists and anthropologists were sure that the origin of man was in Africa and their findings do not give them reason to doubt this. They have been and are still conducting their search and research throughout Africa, specifically in Kenya,

South Africa, Tanganyika, and in Egypt. Some of these findings show that there existed some form of culture as far back as 600,000 years ago in Central Africa.

There is a big gap in history that is hard to fill, as written recordings are a relatively recent development in man's evolution. So we are in the dark when studying the history of certain times; however, we *do know* about the origin of man, and our knowledge is based on the following.

Some of the oldest works of art were found in South Africa and Palestine; they are estimated to be 30,000 years old. Israel, formerly Palestine, was the land of Canaan. The Canaanites were the children of Ham, who was unquestionably Black—they were, therefore, the children of Africa.

The land of Canaan physically adjoins Egypt, which was originally called Mizraim (Mizraim was also one of Ham's sons). To separate Canaan-Palestine-Israel from the African continent is a misconception of which present-day geography is guilty.

Ethiopia was one of the oldest and largest of the civilized empires. Its geographical boundaries at one time extended much farther than they do at present, as can be seen on ancient maps, which also show the South Atlantic as the Ethiopic Ocean. The Ethiopian kings can be traced back to Cush (circa 6200 B.C.), and these kings were Black. Cush was the son of Ham. The kingdom of Cush comprised Ethiopia and the Sudan, and the inhabitants thereof were called Cushites.

The Egyptian civilization goes back thousands of years, as far back as 6,000 B.C. The Ethiopian civilization dates from approximately 7,000 B.C. Incredibly, these civilizations must be considered relatively recent in view of the less heralded civilizations of Kenya, Tanganyika, and Southern Africa.

Can you imagine all the inventions, creations, and works of art that were known so many thousands of years ago? Can you imagine the knowledge that enabled the ancient civilizations to build their vast empires? These we can discuss later on.

Please let us stop for a moment and try to place a little more light on some of the facts mentioned in this chapter, so that we can clear up some potential questions.

I stated that the original man was African, and this has been documented by prominent European scientists.

The New York *Daily News* (January 14, 1967, p. 19) reported that Harvard scientists had discovered human bones in Kenya that were 2.5 million years old.

In the New York *Times* (September 14, 1959, issue) Dr. Louis B. Leakey, a leading anthropologist, reported finding a skull in the Olduvai Gorge in Tanganyika that was approximately 600,000 to 1,000,000 years old. Dr. Leakey's finding was also published in the New York *Daily News* (August 28, 1959, issue).

I have read several history books, written by prominent and renowned historians, which have stated or implied that the origin of man was in places other than Africa; however, I am sure that most of these historians are now aware of the original man and his original home. I have repeated some facts to allow the reader to absorb these important points and to have the opportunity to review them later. Just keep in mind that man lived in Africa 600,000 years ago and possessed the fundamental elements of a culture, as some crude tools were found in that area. (See illustrations and information about the Ethiopian Empire in the *National Geographic*, June 1931, pp. 683, 687, and 690.)

That these empires existed so many thousands of years ago reflects the high level of knowledge and intelligence of man at that time, and this is particularly illustrated by the arts and crafts of wood, metal, and other materials similarly in evidence. Musical instruments were invented, buildings were constructed, and bridges and other forms of construction done. So much of these works of art still puzzle present-day scientists, and they are constantly trying to evaluate them.

In the next chapter, we will discuss some of the ancient accomplishments and contributions that have enabled present-day civilization to be as advanced as it is—for, as we mentioned before, this civilization owes much to the past civilizations of Africa.

2

The Power of the Mind's Eye

Writing history is referring to certain times, people, places, and things; it's quoting historians and elders, referring to discovered items of the past, and recording these observations in an order or sequence that is factual and comprehensive. A good historian reports his findings in a manner that is not boring, and he respects the period of time in reference.

If one decides to write a book or lecture on a contemporary incident or period of time, he need not search too deeply into the past in order to secure his data—and before too long it becomes a matter of compiling words into sentences and putting them into paragraphs. Quite a different task awaits the historian writing the history of Africa and Africans. Where our only source—artifacts—are limited, we have to use a special device. I call this special device the *mind's eye*, which can be defined this way: the mind's eye is that part of the intricate computer—the brain—that takes you back to a scene in order to visualize what has taken place. It takes you to the place that your brain is thinking of. After the brain receives the impulse—the message—the mind's eye takes over and, depending on the issue at hand, expands to present a clearer, more in-depth historical perspective. It is part of the hidden genius that comes alive, alert, and ready; when the brain sends the message, the mind's eye takes over and delves deeper and deeper. Drugs and alcohol blur the brain and do not expand it as so many of us think or are led to believe.

7

The expansion that one may think he is having can be seen as dreams and fantasy.

The best mind tonic is sleep. For instance, when one has a project or problem to solve, he says, "Let me sleep on it"; but he never thinks of the *true* value of sleep. Sometimes in the morning, you awake with a solution to a problem that you could not solve the night before. This is because sleep is more than a rest—it is a period of regrowth for the body. After a good sleep, see how much clearer your mind is and how much better you can think. This is what I mean by a mind tonic.

On the other hand, science shows that when one takes stimulants like alcohol and drugs, he dulls his brain by destroying brain cells. Drugged sleep is not true sleep—*it is not* a period of rejuvenation of the mind. Alcohol and drugs deteriorate the brain, thus deteriorating the mind's eye. Once this occurs, the ability to comprehend, reason, and decipher is handicapped.

To summarize: sleep *restores* the brain; alcohol and drugs *deteriorate* it. In the previous chapter, I tried to review a little of what was said, and, as you no doubt have observed, some of it is repetitious; however, repetition is very necessary to reinforce my message.

Africans were the victims of over one thousand years of abuse, humiliation, and degradation among other things; much of this was due to the attitude that negated the contributions and value of Black people. I don't know how many people are aware of the great annals of Black history; however, as we take the trip by way of the mind's eye to the beginning of life, we will reconstruct this fabulous heritage.

The omnipotent deity, known variously as Ra, God, Iusa, Jehovah, Allah, created this world; he developed light out of the darkness—the sun, which was the lifeline to birth and growth. He created man naked in his own image and likeness and placed man in the area most suitable for survival, which would have to be where the conditions were most ideal—hot days, warm nights, an ample supply of water, and good vegetation.

Keep the mind's eye alert—we are now traveling back a few million years.

Dr. Leakey, a European scientist, found the oldest fossils of man in the cradle of life—in Tanzania—which is in the heart of Africa. There the ideal conditions mentioned above exist.

We now are at the beginning of life. Keeping the mind's eye alert, we can see it will take thousands of years to populate this glorious landmass—one family would have to multiply into many families which in time would result into tribes and villages as we would come to know them.

We can imagine some of the necessities that will arise as the families multiply and spread out, looking for shelter and food among other things. This desire for necessities has always possessed man—as we start off in marriage in a room or a small apartment, and as we have children, we find we need additional space, more food, and other material things; but often our additional needs are not met in the same neighborhood, which causes us to move on to others, and in so doing we encounter different problems in our new environment. So, it is easy to see that our foreparents encountered thousands of years ago similar types of experiences and had to make all types of adjustments— much more than we have to today, for our ancestors did not have the mode of transportation that we now have. They did not even have stores or often shelters, and would thus have to improvise. I hope your mind's eye is following the course of development and progress that is being described. Man, being the genius he is, constantly invented and created to improve his life. When enough people gathered to form a village, a leader necessarily surfaced, just as leaders do today in the cities and nations of the world. As needs and responsibilities in the village multiplied, man met the challenge, using his previous experiences to improvise; and in so doing he became self-educated.

For example, there was a need for rules governing marriage, birth, work, maintenance of the family, property, burial, and many other things. Imagine in your mind's eye the inventions and creations, however simple, that resulted from such a need. Yes, necessity is the mother of invention and creation, and at this point the mind's eye can very well visualize all the things that were necessary to manage a village.

Over hundreds of years, there would be thousands of people

who would spread out into other villages, towns, and cities; problems would become much more complex, as there would be more people to feed, house, clothe, teach, and employ.

Man here had to learn, again out of necessity, how to cut timber, how to cultivate the soil, how to harvest, and how to build and use the products of his knowledge for the benefit of all. The elders became teachers, relating their experiences and imparting knowledge to the younger ones of their communities.

Out of the multiplicity of these things, problems arose, and eventually man had to arrive at some solution or, at the very least, stabilization of these problems. Again, the mind's eye can take you in many directions.

I have traveled through the beginning to this point, by way of the mind's eye, so that we can visualize for ourselves how civilization was constructed.

Do not become bored with my repetition as I go along, as it is very necessary to repeat, if only as an attempt to make up for the centuries-old denial of Black history and culture by force, neglect, and omission. Just as we think of the separate identity of fingerprints, so too is it with man—each with different thoughts, actions, and ideas. With this in mind, one can visualize how these very differences would contribute to the construction of villages, towns, cities, and nations.

Many discoveries are arrived at today by accident—by trial and error. I am sure that many discoveries were arrived at in a similar fashion many thousands of years ago, but, as mentioned previously, *conceiving* of the idea was the genius of the African forefathers. Once they contributed their ideas, civilization had the foundation with which to work, and on which to improvise for thousands of years, resulting in the development of states, empires, and kingdoms as we have come to know them. It is common knowledge that man was created and was born without clothes, and this was his natural state in the "cradle" of Tanzania; but as man evolved and moved in all directions away from the cradle, he encountered different temperatures and, out of necessity, was forced to come up with some type of cover. At first, this was probably nothing more than a fig leaf. However, it did not take man long to realize that this item would not last very long, and as a result he learned how to separate and mat together fibers from different trees, presupposing the manufacture of cloth. As you and I know, man—never being content with what he has—kept on improving this item. You have only to look around today to see this.

Just as some of us have gifts or talents that no one can explain, so had the African forefathers. Using their knowledge, they developed areas of specialty. For example, after several births in a particular village, certain individuals would be thought of as possessing great skill and knowledge in the delivery of children. These individuals, then, would become experts in the most important phase of human development. So too in time would there be experts in fishing, hunting, farming, building, and all the things that your mind's eye can think of, all the things that necessity engendered. As I mentioned previously, these experts would eventually become teachers of their knowledge and experiences; after several generations of transmitting experiences, the communal knowledge broadened and an improved society resulted.

I do hope I have stimulated your mind's eye so that you can at least partially understand how the African forefathers contributed CIVILIZATION TO THE WORLD.

Between the time of creation at the cradle in Tanzania and up to his present phase of development, man has been through all types of activities, millions of thoughts, ideas, accidental discoveries, inventions by trial and error, and many other things, which, of course, continue to stimulate him due to his curious nature and restlessness. The "magic" of healing is one such area that has stimulated man.

I mentioned the medicine man earlier. He started out like all the other experts, out of necessity, and had to improve with time and experience.

Just imagine a baby, yours or someone else's, having some form of difficulty with a cold, a broken limb, a cut, fever, stomach pains, or some other ailment; you can almost feel the pain, and you are very upset, but you don't know what to do. There is no doctor's office down the street, no clinic; you continue to get desperate, and others in the family are called. You get much consolation and sympathy and are told all types of things like "don't worry," "everything will be all right," "it will pass," "it will heal." Some may even pray and meditate, but up to this point, no physical help comes forth. I stated previously that people are like fingerprints—all very different. In this situation, a relative shows up who is different—he does not watch or pray. He does a *physical* thing—he picks up the baby and takes him outside. He wipes the sweat off, cleans the nostrils, bathes the infant, gives him water to drink. He may rub the infant's stomach for the pain there, put sand or mud on the wound, but whatever he does is comforting to the parents, even if the results are only a fifty percent improvement. The mere fact that this relative *did* something positive is what really mattered—the family is happy, relieved, and thankful. You can imagine that when similar incidents occur, the family will call on this person over and over again. He will learn, as does every one else, from his experiences, make mistakes, and correct them in future cases—but he will be *depended* on, that's for sure.

The same factors that today motivate doctors to improve their treatment are the same ones that motivated our forefathers —the physician builds his knowledge and ability by the feedback he gets from his patients, which motivates him to learn more to do better, thus enabling him to remain at the top of the field.

The person mentioned before who came forward and contributed his services could have been the one whom we would today call gifted. He would be looked up to. Again, in the course of time, he would become an elder and a teacher of his experiences. His learning would be passed on for generations, and the result would be the medicine man—the precursor of today's M.D.

It is interesting to note that many of the medicines used thousands of years ago are being used by today's doctors—herbs, barks, fibers, and roots augmented by psychology are all components of medical treatment today. There are modifications and improvisions, that's for sure, but no one can deny that we are using our forefathers' knowledge. Medicine as we know it has undergone big changes, particularly in the twentieth century, due to the aid of technology—specifically through complex electronic devices. However, let us suppose that there are no devices. We would then see the M.D., for all practical purposes, reverting back to the bush doctor. You can further visualize this by using your mind's eye. Imagine a visit to your doctor's office. There is no blood pressure gauge, no stethoscope, heart, or X ray machine —there are just the two of you and the furniture! You describe your illness to the doctor, and he must now examine you. He would have to employ body contact to listen to your heart, take your pulse, look into your eyes, and complete his examination. On completion of the examination, he would have to give advice and possibly a prescription. He would have few patented medicines and would mix his own herbs, roots, and oils, or you might be sent to a "pharmacist" who would do the same.

Many doctors are reverting to the ancient medicines of roots, herbs, and fibers, which were used by the African forefathers.

Some writers have pointed out that within mummified Egyptians were found abscesses, gall stones, burst appendices, solidification of the lung, and other illnesses. Their conclusion, therefore, was that the Egyptians could not have known very much about medicine. This statement is clearly ridiculous, because even now in the twentieth century many people are suffering and dying from the same ailments. Does this imply that modern doctors do not know anything about medicine?

As I have already stated, repetition is necessary so that we can understand how our forefathers contributed to the natural sciences, this time the science of medicine. Medical records several thousand years old have been found in Africa, and you will become knowledgeable about them.

Consider this item: what we have come to know as a musical instrument may have been derived out of necessity. After man drifted away from the cradle (hunting may have been the cause for this), his communication by vision and the sound of his voice became limited. At first, man would send and receive sound signals by tapping sticks together. The he tapped bamboo reeds together, which had a higher sound, and later moved on to another primitive instrument, which we today call the drum. Originally, the drum may have been a hollow tree trunk, subject to further improvisations. As the world knows, Africans used and still use the drums for communication, ceremonial functions, and for entertainment.

Man developed the flute from the very same bamboo reeds, and possibly the stringed instruments were the result of the humming noise of the bow that was used to launch the arrow when hunting.

Your mind's eye is now as wild as my own in visualizing how the African forefathers contributed much more to civilization than we could possibly think of. You should be so alert and involved in African history that it would be impossible for you to become bored. When you read or heard of the history of Africa and Africans, you have probably ignored it. In the past, the mind's eye was asleep from lack of concern; it was drugged by alcohol, by narcotics, and in depressed states by means of intimidation and humiliation, mostly because of slavery, colonial indoctrination, dehumanization, and ignorance. These are but a few obstacles that have stopped some Africans at home and abroad from making their full contribution to civilization. I say some because contributions *were* made even under the most horrible conditions. For example, witness the marvelous contributions of George Washington Carver, among others, despite the severe conditions and circumstances of slavery that he and so many others encountered. I mentioned Carver because he is one that many of us were allowed to know of—but there are many others, which I have every intention of mentioning. Yes, the mind's eye is alert.

Many Africans were turned off like short-circuited light switches and thrown into darkness in panic and fear—disorganized and disoriented. However, the time has come to repair the switch and turn the light on, and to keep a steady vigil over the switch. Open up your mind's eye! Prepare yourself to do anything and everything to prevent the switch from being turned off again.

Just as we scan the past with the mind's eye, so too may we

scan the future. However, let's not get ahead, looking into the future, while we are still looking back hundreds of thousands of years.

While out seeking food, man got involved in catching fish in the rivers and ponds. He probably caught fish by snatching them out of the water, but then the fish would learn to stay away from the banks of the river, and this caused him to go into the water after them. This could not have lasted long, since the fish learned to get away. Man then resorted to his oldest tool—the rock—to throw at the fish; this, too, had its limitations. (Keep in mind that man had plenty of time, and that time, even today, is one of the biggest factors in accomplishing any objective.) The African later used sticks to try and catch the sealife, but after using all these devices, the fish would be driven away, and man would soon realize that *he* chased them away and would have to try something else to capture them.

Either by accident or design, man might have floated a tree trunk or branch onto the water, thereby gaining a better vantage point from which to fish. In the course of time, again through necessity, he would improve on this crude floating object, thus doing any number of things to make it much more comfortable to operate. He would learn to balance and would learn to control movement of the logs with the very same sticks that he was using to stab the fish. Over hundreds of years of improvising this crude object, man would develop what we today term a boat, which would make him, in addition to being a hunter or fisherman, a traveler.

As we all know, traveling into an unknown area is an experience that a million words cannot explain thoroughly. A man would learn to swim, suffer sea sickness, and observe different types of fish. He would also learn that water would be deeper in one area than another, and that the rivers, seas, and oceans were new avenues of knowledge and reward.

I am sure that your mind's eye can focus on things that I did not mention. These experiences—such as sailing to new lands and coping with new environments—led me to mention earlier than man developed his habitat out of necessity, through the multiplicity of ideas, thoughts, and discoveries, whether by accident or through ingenuity. He has never stopped evolving even to this day. If you can read anything else into what I am saying, your insight is entirely welcome.

In the last 2,000 years, and especially in the last 600, many Africans have fallen into slumber, either by complacency or systematic design, and have stopped using that part of the world's greatest computer—the mind's eye. This was the cause of the deterioration and eventual discontinuation of African empire building, which diminished the African contributions to civilization. Do not get the idea, however, that Africans did not make contributions to civilization in this period; it would be a great tragedy to think so. It is just that during this period many Africans were in the process of "going to sleep," either by complacency or design.

To prevent a misunderstanding at a future point in this book, let us review some of the documented contributions made by Africans during the worst period of these several hundred years of dethroning, particularly the many years of colonial subjugation.

Consider the following eye-opener: sometime during the first century, the African prophet Jesus Christ was born. This prophet revolutionized religion and reshaped the world's actions and thoughts.

Less than one hundred years ago, another child of Africa made a most startling and needed contribution. This man was Jan Matzeliger, and he developed the shoe-making machine in September 1891. Can anyone deny the importance of this contribution?

Between the time of Christ and Jan Matzeliger, there were flourishing civilizations in Songay and Zimbabwe, among others. Could you imagine the contributions other Africans could have made if their mind's eye had been alert?

Let's get back now to how the great contributions of African culture came about. The contributions started with the elders and teachers, who would get together and share their ideas, discoveries, and opinions. There would be a combination of trades and talents put together, so that over several hundred years the community would advance; so over ten thousand years, the society's progress would be quite significant and would continue to advance.

One member of Dr. Leakey's staff, P. Nuzube (an African), discovered one of the oldest human skulls in the cradle of Tanganyika, now called Tanzania. This skull was determined to be over two million years old. There were no records and the artifacts of this period are few, basically some crude stone tools. This is why we have to ask, "What was happening two million years ago? What did the African forefathers look like? Exactly what did they do? What did they eat, and what were their dwellings?" Until we get the artifacts—the clues—to open these two million years of mystery, we must use the mind's eye to examine this period. We are sure, definitely, positively, and absolutely beyond reasonable doubt, that the inhabitants were Africans and that they were Black.

To summarize this chapter: man evolved over several hundred thousand years from families to nations, and out of necessity he developed several skills and talents; and from the artifacts of some very early stone cultures, we know he moved north from Tanzania. Also, in this chapter I tried to elaborate and expand on how hunting came about, for this very necessary activity of survival initiated subsequent progress.

The medicine man, as we came to know him, resulted from trial and error attempts to relieve pain and suffering—artifacts support this. Construction and all the related talents were derived from man's need to protect himself from the elements and later to afford greater comfort.

Education was developed through the elders' passing on all their knowledge and experiences from generation to generation. This is still a tradition in many tribes today; for example, in some tribes it is still necessary for youngsters, during their manhood training, to recite their history, family tree, and related facts. (Indeed, how different is the above from our concept of university education?) All of the elders' contributions can make us see how it would be necessary in time to have a leader, or leaders, sort and collate all of the transmitted knowledge and use it for the benefit of the society. It is easy to see that the leaders, entrusted with the collation and dissemination of knowledge, would eventually become known as *government*.

Keep in mind that the administration, or government, would see many improvisions, through the thousands of years, and also keep in mind that a few thousand years of development is not a long time in relation to the discovery of man over two million years ago. Man did develop, as recently discovered artifacts show, and came to contribute several civilizations, which we will discuss in later chapters. Most of these civilizations will make the mind's eye of all men, particularly Blacks, glow with pride. Africa's children were at work then, at work now, and will always be at work improving our civilizations.

3

The Great Vision

I do hope I have stirred your curiosity enough in the previous chapters to cause you to challenge the facts therein presented. For, as I've said, it is common and normal for this to be done.

It is possible, too, that you may accept the facts because you know them to be correct; if this is so, I am proud. However, I feel that one should challenge those things that leave questions in the mind. We discussed the original man and his origin, and I tried to demonstrate how his environment evolved, and how he developed culture and civilization. As you will come to understand, this took some doing.

The origin of man may not seem interesting at first, but as you read along, it captures your interest and makes you involved in the most sustaining issue of the universe—the original people, Africans.

Herodotus, the Greek historian of the fifth century B.C., had much to say about his amazement upon seeing Africa. He noted that the natives in Egypt and the surrounding countries of that area were black with woolly hair. He was particularly impressed with their standards of civilization—a civilization that existed well over two thousand years before our time. Herodotus observed the land long before many modern nations—such as Germany, Austria, France, Poland, and Switzerland—came into existence.

Man's life-style evolved, as was stated before, into tribal life, which became village governments; as the villages multiplied, they became citylike governments, which eventually developed into kingdoms and other sophisticated forms of government.

It took thousands of years for man to change his environment; it is quite ironic that this change can be explained in minutes by just skipping thousands of years. What's more, a leap in time is often necessitated by a lack of records, which makes reconstruction of any given period impossible. Even if a report could be given on each and every government, it would prove tedious and boring. As pointed out in the beginning of this book, I have not written a major work in evolution—such a study would necessarily have to span many centuries in an in-depth manner, and this was not my intention.

No one can give an accurate account of time from the beginning to the present, but there are those things that stand out, that we cannot help but study and elaborate on. I will now state some of the facts known about the previous civilizations of Africa's children.

CULTURES

The oldest cultures that we know of were in Kenya, Southern Africa, Tanganyika, Chad, Egypt, and Ethiopia. Now keep in mind that repetition is essential to clarify various points.

Using the mind's eye, try to think of a culture that existed in 100,000 B.C. to 50,000 B.C. to 10,000 B.C. In the culture of 100,000 B.C., man was believed to be naked. As was mentioned before, the environment did not require man to wear clothes, and therefore he was not motivated to develop clothes. However, he had a shelter and crude tools and probably was still near the cradle of Tanganyika. He hunted, fished, and reared a family, and we must assume that this was his way of life. Between 50,000 and 30,000 B.C., he had improved his culture very much.

The artifacts show that art, such as carvings and paintings, were added, which greatly improved communications, and, of course, later allowed scientists and historians to understand some of the actions and thoughts of that period of time. At this point, the Black man started recording his thoughts and actions pictorially, which led to other forms of communication.

I am sure that you have heard the expressions, "Africa the dark continent, the uncivilized continent with naked people"; such expressions were inaccurate and served to defame Africa and in turn all her children. But there was more than defamation involved—there was an insidious intent to rewrite history, removing the stigma of dark continent from Europe, and shifting this dubious title to Africa and her children. I am telling it like it is and was. A few honest historians admitted that this assertion is correct; however, the majority distorted history by trying to put Europe in the vanguard of history. Try to understand that I am saying that Europe was the barbaric continent, that its people were still living in caves when Africa was in her glory with civilized empires in Ethiopia, Egypt, the Congo, Zimbabwe, and Cush, among others. Europe, at that time, was comprised of Greece, Spain, Rome, and France—the remainder was claimed by ice.

No one can take from Africa and her children the glory of being the beginning of civilization and the contributors of what followed after. Africa and her children were the creators of art, music, science, religion, law, the alphabet, mathematics, medicine, astrology, and on and on. The great inventions and technological advances, such as mining and manufacturing of essential materials, were responsible for the evolution of civilization. Wood, gold, iron, paper, cloth, cut stone, and bricks were contributed by the African forefathers.

My intention is not to distort history but instead to tell it like it is and was, regardless of where it may lead us.

It is true that the Greeks made some form of contribution to civilization, and it is true that the Romans and other Europeans did so too; however, their contributions came centuries after the African empires had already made theirs. The Greek, Roman, and early European cultures had to go to Africa to learn the skills, trades, and sciences. Historians, therefore, cannot lay claim that these cultures are the fathers of law, medicine, religion, and the sciences. All these advances belong—definitely, positively, absolutely, and beyond any reasonable doubt—to Africa and all her Black children. Yes, today's Blacks are the descendants of such people who greatly shaped civilization. Their legacy of arts, crafts, and writings is a testimony to their pride, resourcefulness, intelligence, and, of course, their beauty.

Blacks today have a great responsibility—they must ensure that Africa's children understand their heritage and history. They must perpetuate a study of African ancestry, which has been denied for so long.

Consider this exercise for the mind's eye: Hippocrates, we are told, is the father of medicine—but how can this be so? Medicine was being practiced in Africa thousands of years before Hippocrates was born.

There was previous mention of a culture that existed in Southern Africa and Israel some 30,000 years before Christ. Both areas are located on the African continent. (As I have previously pointed out, the placement of Israel-Palestine-Canaan in Asia is not correct, or even rational. The area has changed names throughout the centuries, but the geography remains the same—the area adjoins Egypt.)

The culture of which I am speaking featured paintings, and this involved other things—for example, the paints had to be *made*, which indicates a high level of culture. Upon arriving at paint manufacture, man became involved in the early forms of chemistry, the mixture of oils and barks; but where did man get the oils and barks, and what did the "artists" do to make their paint endure 30,000 years? Use your mind's eye.

Evidence of the art done 30,000 years ago can be found in the book *Africa's Gift to America*, written by the able and prominent historian J. A. Rogers, not to mention all the other historical facts that can be found in his book. This book features a picture of the greatest piece of African art—the work dates back some 30,000 years!

Now if such works of art were done by Africans 30,000 years ago, let us try to visualize the various contributions made and the scientific ability that followed. It has been repeatedly stated that Africans have contributed little if any to civilization, and if we look around us, it is hard to refute this allegation. However, if we go back and try to "link up" to the past, maybe we can arrive at the glory of Black history.

USE THE MIND'S EYE

The African ancestors lived in caves, tents, straw huts, mud huts, and shelters of this type, until they learned how to measure, cut, and assemble stone, and until they arrived at the scientific way of mining clay and making it into bricks. Then they developed the ability to assemble these bricks and stone with such precision that not even 6,000 years of time have been able to make them fall. It may seem insignificant at first, but use your mind's eye again—if all the brick and stone that are used around us were not here, what would life be like? Consider that for a moment! Think now of the constructions of brick and stone that surround you.

The Great African fathers learned how to use wood—think of the *absence* of all the things made of wood around you and what it would be like without them. Just consider that for a moment! No floors, ceilings, or doors, and no furniture, among other things.

The African fathers mined iron with their scientific ingenuity. They had to discover that iron ore was in the earth and had to know how to separate it from the earth and smelt it, and then put it into different forms. Keep in mind that they had to make furnaces and molds, which required scientific knowledge. Now think of the world without iron. There would be no bridges, skyscrapers, subways, or tunnels; there would be no automobiles, trucks, or trains, and neither would there be a thousand other by-products of iron.

Use your mind's eye and try to visualize the surroundings without works of stone, without brick, without wood, and without iron—it would almost be like a wilderness—wouldn't you say that? We would be back to the days when life was on the open plain, a hut here and there.

You may say, forget the iron—there is steel and aluminum,

and tin, and so forth; but as I stated before, these are by-products of an original discovery. You could not manufacture these metals without first learning the science of smelting.

I do hope you are beginning to see the great value of the contributions made by the African fathers for us, the benefits of which we take for granted, and the comforts of which the whole world enjoys. Yes, the African forefathers did all this for us and much, much, more, so let us not forsake the great forefathers.

I mentioned in the previous chapter that there is a gap in Black history that is hard to fill, due to the fact that writing systems did not exist at certain periods, and records were represented through drawings and similar forms of art. I have tried to scan the events of this gap with my mind's eye.

The ancient Egyptians developed one of mankind's greatest tools—writing—which was achieved through hieroglyphics (pictures and signs conveying meaningful elements). In time, it became necessary to have something on which to record hieroglyphics, so another great scientific achievement was arrived at—this time papyrus, or paper. The Egyptians used the reeds of the papyrus plant to make paper. Try to visualize what the world would be like without writing, or even without paper to write on. We would still be living in the historical gap without records.

Through these accomplishments in historical recording, our brothers in Africa were able to leave some of the history of these great achievements, so as to teach us how to challenge the years hence. The real reason, then, for the search for artifacts is not just to find out how old they are but instead to find the technology that motivated the world's geniuses.

What I have said so far, then, is that Africa and Africans contributed not just to a particular civilization but instead contributed civilization *to the world*. Just to emphasize some contributions, and I really do think they need emphasizing, the African forefathers contributed the months of the year and the seasons; they contributed writing and paper; they contributed music and instruments, the science of medicine and law, and orderly governments of people. They contributed religion, art, astronomy, and astrology. The African fathers also contributed the sciences of making gold, silver, copper, iron, bricks, cut stone, cement, wood, as well as the art of using these products. They contributed the sciences of warfare on land and on sea; they were great historians, poets, and writers; they contributed the wheel; they domesticated animals; they farmed and discovered the irrigation system. Yes, they contributed all these things and still more. Their greatest contribution, however, was the sum total of their achievements—*civilization.* There never was and never can be a greater contribution than civilization.

My motive here is to make you see that the Empire State Building, the United Nations Building, the White House, the schools and all the furnishings, and even the home you live in would not be here if it were not for the contributions of the African forefathers. From this day on remember that the African civilizations were the beginning . . . and what a glorious beginning it was! All who came after those civilizations made some contributions also, but they just experimented, improvised, and improved on the original ones. We are happy to know of all the other breakthroughs made on the original inventions and discoveries, and we respect others for this. All that Africa's children want is respect and recognition for their forefathers' original inventions and discoveries. I hope I have begun to interest you in the glory of the African fathers. If you are stirred in motion, you will certainly become emotionally involved and go out and discover more than I did—for there are more ways and means to do so now than before.

I will explain how and where some of the information mentioned here can be found, and why it is written in a certain manner in some of the books.

When the phrase "Black is Beautiful" is used, try to see it in the light—it is not just the beauty of the person only, but also the beauty of the genius of the African race. Being African is being original—did you not notice the attempt to be African

in Algeria, Rhodesia, Angola, and in Monomotapa (alias South
Africa)? The Europeans in these nations changed their identity
to *African*; but in so doing, they changed Africa's children to
coloreds, natives, and other demeaning identities. Use your mind's
eye and ask one question—WHY? Why did they want to change
their identity? Only your mind's eye can explain this to you.
Remember, do not fail to investigate why some Europeans would
want to claim that they are Africans.

4

Setting the Record Straight

As we start another chapter of our history, I hope that you are deeply involved, that you have checked on the facts mentioned, and that you have quelled even the slightest doubt. This may be done by conducting research in books, libraries, and museums.

This history is the hidden treasure, the absence of which limits the ability of Blacks to achieve any objective in the universe—it is their pride and dignity, and their hidden genius. Once the mind's eye focuses on the greatest contribution ever made to the world, which is civilization and all the scientific discoveries and inventions that were necessary to form this contribution, there will be no limit on Black achievement.

The African forefathers made and left these contributions, and the world presently enjoys the ensuing comforts. Now, Blacks have to make their contributions by unlocking the closed doors of this history, so that in conjunction with their children they can continue the partly interrupted cycle of Black contributions. We hope to insure that every generation, from now on, will be able to look back at their history. Before I get along in explaining how and where some of the facts mentioned in the last chapter can be found, I would like to make a few points.

I have no intention of insulting my readers' intelligence, but some of you are not thoroughly aware of the geography of Africa, as it relates to the history of past centuries. It is true that some know it as it is shown today, and some may know it better than I can explain it. I must begin by saying that Egypt is in Africa and at the time of the great history I speak of, the Egyptians were Black. The proof of this can be seen in pictures and recorded history. However, I will give you a hint.

In *Earlier Ages*, Prof. James Henry Breasted points out that the Sphinx is the portrait of Khafre, who, together with his son, Khufu, built the first and second of the three great pyramids.

In his writings, Herodotus (c. 484-425 B.C.) observes that the Egyptians were Black with woolly hair. In *Africa's Gift to America*, by J. A. Rogers, the distinct features of Africa's children are associated with the Sphinx. Indeed, one has only to look at any photo of the Sphinx at Giza to see the distinct features of Africa's children.

The land of Canaan, presently called Israel, adjoins Egypt and is hence part of Africa. The Canaanites were Africa's children—that is, they were the children of Ham, who was Black. Ham's other children were Mizraim (Egypt), Cush (Ethiopia and the Sudan), and Put or Punt (Somalia and Arabia).

Historians have written of the fertile crescent, but did you realize that the inhabitants of this area were children of Africa? Recorded history does not lie.

It is important to note that the Middle East is peopled by Africa's children and that the area is a part of the African continent. You will be able to see this if you keep your mind's eye alert.

To find proof of all the contributions made by Black people is very difficult, since the records and other objects that were salvaged are scattered all over the world in libraries, museums, and other such places. To obtain all this information personally would require a lot of time and money. However, there is much information around if you will just take a few minutes a day to search and read. If I mention well-documented books written by Black men, this may tend to make one have doubts; so instead, I will recommend some books written by Europeans.

Let us start our search for proof of the facts mentioned in the previous chapters. We will first start with medicine.

The Story of Medicine, written by Dr. Victor Robinson, states that the oldest medical records yet discovered came from Egypt, dating from 2160 to 1788 B.C. He also states the existence of the Surgical Papyrus, which was written about 1600 B.C. In this document, which was over fifteen feet in length and was written in black ink, the various medical problems of Egypt were diagnosed and methods of curing them mentioned. Furthermore, Dr. Robinson explains that the papyrus mentioned before was a copy of the original, which had been written 1,000 years before—in 2600 B.C.!

Dr. Robinson also comments on *The Book on Surgery and External Medicine,* an Egyptian document that actually defines Egyptian medicine as it was practiced 4,500 years ago. Of course, there is so much more to be learned from Dr. Robinson's book.

Another book on medicine is *How to Live with Diabetes,* written by Henry Dolger, M.D., and Bernard Seeman. This book points out that almost 3,500 years ago, Egyptian doctors had diagnosed diabetes and prescribed certain diets for diabetes sufferers.

Hieroglyphics, the first writing, was contributed by the Egyptians, or the Ethiopians, and then modified by the Phoenicians. F. J. Aspenleiter, in his book *Western Civilizations,* shows that hieroglyphic writing was contributed by the Egyptians and modified by the Phoenicians. Paper and ink, mathematics and literature, history and science, agriculture and industry, and the establishment of religion were also contributed by the Egyptians. Aspenleiter places the age of metal as early as 5000 B.C. in the Mediterranean area. I must point out that African civilization was in bloom in 5000 B.C.

In his book, J. F. Horrabim points out, through the use of maps, that iron was being exported from Zimbabwe, which is presently called Rhodesia, in the twelfth century A.D.

There are many books not mentioned here that give much added information. One of these books points out that the Egyptians introduced the calendar. The author indirectly mentions the discovery and use of metals, such as copper, tin, and bronze. He goes on to say that the people of Western Europe became acquainted with iron only in the last thousand years—and this only after contact with the African civilizations.

Herodotus wrote that the Egyptians he personally saw were Black, as were the Phoenicians, the Carthagenians, and the Moors. He also wrote that Africa had flourishing empires when Greece and Rome were not yet born.

As a shortcut to history and historical records, I mention here some of the books written by J. A. Rogers—his facts are well documented, and his books feature many pictures and works of art. The following books are recommended:

1. *World's Great Men of Color*
2. *From Superman to Man*
3. *Sex and Race*
4. *100 Amazing Facts about the Negro*

Many historians have pointed out at various times that Europe was in a barbaric state when Africa was in her glory with civilized empires. They further point out that Africans went to Europe and contributed to civilizing the people there, and this went on as late as A.D. 500. The Blacks brought the alphabet, metals, cloth, pottery, and various works of art to the Europeans, and nurtured them into civilization.

Herodotus has much to say on the many contributions made by the Blacks to civilization. Much of Greek and Roman civilizations was similar to that of the African cultures. I am not downgrading the Greeks or Romans—but I am just telling it like it is. These civilizations contributed very little to what was already there. They modified existing art and technology but made no major breakthroughs in original discoveries and inventions.

Now, as we review, it would seem as though all the great contributions were made in the northernmost part of Africa—particularly Egypt; however, this is not true, because there were great civilized empires, as recently discovered ruins show, in the Congo, in Zimbabwe, in Sudan, in Ghana, Nigeria, and Ethiopia, just to name a few.

The belief in the existence of advanced African civilizations has been plagued by open-ended statements. I define an open-ended statement as one that can be interpreted in many ways. It leads your mind's eye this way and that, without saying anything definite. An example of an open-ended statement that is frequently used is "the people of the Mediterranean Sea area were the contributors of civilization to the world." This statement is an open-ended statement because the Mediterranean area is vast and includes countries in Europe as well as Africa. Therefore, we could be talking about Italy and Greece as much as we could about Egypt. We, therefore, are not led to believe that the contributors of civilization were Africa's children. This is the essence of such a statement. Look carefully; it says nothing specific. Ask yourself which group of people were the contributors of civilization, and see if the statement answers it. I hope this makes my point.

Artifacts show some form of arithmetic in the Congo as far back as 6000 B.C. The civilization in Zimbabwe was mining iron and gold thousands of years ago; Sudan was manufacturing cloth hundreds of years ago; and the domestication of animals and the development of sophisticated agriculture in Southern Africa long presupposed similar achievements elsewhere. Do not be led to believe that civilization started in the Middle East, as this area is identified, for this is erroneous and misleading. The artifacts show, as was pointed out before, that there was civilization in other African states. However, most emphasis is placed on the artifacts of Egypt. Two good reasons for this are the Western predilection to keep the birth of civilization in the Mediterranean Sea area and the finding of numerous artifacts in the Nile delta region. But these views must not be allowed to blot out the civilizations in the Central and Southern parts of Africa. Africa was the nucleus of life. This life, in the course of time, spread east, west, north, and south out of the middle of this glorious continent, disseminating history, art, and culture.

Remember, the birth of man was in the center of Africa, and the birth of civilization and all the things that make a civilization was in the heart of Africa. Do not forget that God created man in his own image and likeness, which unquestionably means that God is an African; He is Black. Some may laugh at this; they may not want to accept it, even though it is documented—it is written in so many books of authority. I am sure that, after you think these historical facts through, and read any of the books with this information, you will be convinced that this is correct.

Remember that Christ is depicted through European eyes. This means that the Father is also seen as a European. Again, you may laugh at this statement, but when you have the time to think of this and of how this assertion was enforced in books, and particularly how it has hurt Africa's children physically, socially, and psychologically, you will not laugh at this anymore. The damage was done by exclusively showing Christ as a European and by leaving Blacks with no history, no mother country, no identity to hold them together, and no background for them to be proud of. But this can no longer be hidden; all the artifacts show that Africans were the beginning. All the pictures and statutes of antiquity show the Gods, regardless of political or religious persuasion, to be African in image—including those in Europe.

One European novelist wrote recently that the construction of some of the great wonders of the world—like the Sphinx and the Pyramids in Egypt, the Great Stone culture at the Easter Islands, and the gigantic stone heads in South America—were all African images. The author stated that they were done hundreds of years ago but could not have been done by the Africans, because they were not intelligent enough. This author feels that people from other planets came to enlighten the African forefathers—and constructed the various monuments. Use your mind's eye. Why did they, the visitors, make all these images with African features? At this point, I wish that you do not read any further until you have given serious thought to this novelist's attempt to distort the facts.

5

Putting It Together

In the past chapters, I have tried to get the individual to become involved, not just to read but instead to become really involved, in learning about the great heritage of Blacks. I have tried to make us all involved by using words more relative to everyday life, words that do not require too much thinking or research. The purpose for this is that everyone, educated or not, can participate and learn at the same time the values of the greatest contribution—*civilization*—and of all the things it entailed. Please accept my repetition as a necessity.

As Blacks, Africans were the original people—the great movers of civilization—how is it that Africa's children are in such a deprived state today?

In the physical sense, Africa's children are still the same gifted beings, but they are enslaved by a limited knowledge of self. They do not know their history and hence cannot motivate the genius within their minds. The purpose of this book, as previously stated, is to *awaken* Africa's children to the limitless capacity of their genius. When the mental abilities unite with the physical, then Africa's children will reclaim their original status.

You will become mentally alert if you continue to do what was previously mentioned to keep your mind's eye alive and healthy, but no one can actually do this for you. When the mental capacity meets the physical, then you will be on the right track to making your contribution.

Just about anything you can think about today will take you back to the African continent and the Black ancestors. Just think of paper, cloth, metals, music, religion, literature, medicine, or science—all the things I have pointed out in previous chapters, showing that they were original ideas that required a high level of intelligence and determination.

Let me try to show that the original ideas contributed by the African fathers move the world today. The light bulb was invented in 1879, but this could not have been accomplished without the original contribution of glass; electricity was discovered, but this could not have been done without metals; television was invented, but this could not have been done without the use of electricity, metal, glass, etc., the spaceship was invented and will soon be piloted to other planets, but this could not have been accomplished without the original knowledge of astronomy, metal, wood, paper, cloth, glass, etc. As you can see, civilization today advances on the basis of the great contributions made by the African forefathers. I state all this to bring our thoughts closer to the reality of the great contribution of civilization itself.

I mentioned in the previous chapters that it is possible today, if one will take a little time, to go out and dig up some of this history without much effort. One very convenient source of this type of information is the American Museum of Natural History in New York—particularly the African exhibit, which points out the origin of man in Africa and some of the contributions made by the Americans to civilization. Your observations of Black heritage in the museum will be more interesting after you have read this book. I have repeatedly mentioned that Blacks have contributed civilization to the world—had they not been interrupted, mankind could very well be living in a more advanced state of life today. The world has been able to advance only to the level of the civilization developed by the African forefathers. Yes, after receiving all the contributions of Black civilization, and by compiling, sorting, and then experimenting with all the discoveries and improvisations, man has been able to advance to the peak level of African civilization.

Every applied idea and invention is hundreds of years in the making, as was mentioned before. I have pointed this out so as to tie the past centuries to the present and to show that the conception of inventions thousands of years ago required as much, if not more, intelligence than is presently needed. Because there were fewer inventions from which to copy, the forefathers, therefore, had to work that much harder and had to be that much more creative. We must keep in mind that our complex technology is largely based on fundamental discoveries and inventions by the African civilizations. Our technology, then, is a refinement and improvisation of original breakthroughs, and for this the improvisers must be praised—but they could not improvise on an item had it not been previously discovered or invented. These must be kept in mind when speaking of the previous inventions and discoveries of Africa's children. It is worthy to note here that you should read about some of the inventions of Africa's children in the Americas. You see these inventions everyday and yet are not aware of them. Read the book *Black Inventors of America*, by McKinley Burt, Jr., and I am sure you will be quite shocked.

In the next chapter, we will try to trace the Black heritage down to the present through the trails of thousands of years and will also try to put the broken chain together. We will arrive at some very sad and humiliating days and years, however. But I have promised to tell the truth, regardless of where it may lead us—whether to glory or to pain.

I hope that my readers, after having completed this book, will be able to bury the misnomers *nigger* and *negro* forever, and will thus use the rightful identity of *African*. It is essential that both Blacks and whites cultivate this distinction in cultural heritage.

6

On the Trail

In this chapter of history, let us consider where Blacks came from and some of the trails they have traveled from the beginning to the twentieth century—from somewhere in Kenya, Tanzania, Angola, Namabia, the Congo, Uganda, Ethiopia, Sudan, Ghana, Egypt, or even through Israel, Jordan, or Arabia, which were all extentions of Africa before it was divided by the mapmakers. All the way along these trails, civilizations were built by the African fathers. Along some of these trails there are remnants of the artifacts of civilization—the greatest contribution the world has ever known.

A civilization entails many skills, trades, professions, and various types of materials, and the evidence shows that they were there. When you investigate Roman and Greek culture, you will learn that Africans contributed to the building of those civilizations and others like them in Europe. Africans were in North and South America before Columbus had a hundred grandfathers, and they contributed to the civilizations there— these facts have been reported by prominent historians, and there are artifacts that can prove this beyond controversy.

In previous chapters, it has been pointed out that it was impossible to explain history in detail from the beginning, year by year, because of the absence of various forms of communication in the beginning. Even when art was expressed on rocks, tablets, and parchments, and the early forms of writing were recorded, most of this was lost or eroded by time. Some were willfully destroyed, some were lost by wars, and others were lost by acts of nature—for instance, conflagrations or floods. Still, there were enough extant records and artifacts to pass down the life of several millennia to us.

Today we are searching and researching the past. The giant is coming alive in the children of Africa. The words *nigger* and *negro*, which are slave terms, have been nearly eradicated. Africa's children all over the world are now "Black and proud." Blacks no longer hide their lips or pinch their noses; rather, they are expressing their features to the full.

The call to Africa's children is: "Wake up, you mighty genius and start using your mind's eye. Express why you are Black, beautiful, and proud." The history and culture of Africa and her children will create a unity that will enable Blacks to move forward with unparalleled success.

It is now time for Blacks to live up to their African identity. Remember, African is original. Blacks must not allow anyone to remove their African identity—it is their connection to pride and dignity, the greatest link in their being. The strength of nations lies within this link. Use your mind's eye and examine what has just been said. I'm sure you will agree.

Once you become awake to the riches of Black heritage, you will never fall asleep again, and since you will stay awake, you will not settle for knowing just what I know. You will go out and look, question, and visualize. Blacks will be happy from within and will then begin to know why they should be proud and what the phrase "Black Is Beautiful" is all about. Only when Africa's children can feel this from within will their hidden genius come alive, which will enable them to move on to higher planes, to continue the nation building that was interrupted several hundred years ago. For the most part, this interruption was due to slavery.

THE MISNOMER SLAVERY

There are no nice words to describe slavery, and there are no words terrible enough to denounce slavery. The despicable life of slavery is without definition. How can one explain the trauma as a result of torture, intimidation, humiliation, degradation, deprivation, starvation, dehumanization, and assassination perpetrated upon mankind by man? How can one just simply call it slavery? The legal definition of slavery is working without just compensation, but the indignities do not fit the definition. As many as 100 million of Africa's children were captured, crated, and chained like animals and submitted to nameless tortures and terror. Many died as a result; some committed suicide rather than submit to the ghastliest of crimes; others jumped overboard in attempts to escape the slave ships. Still more of our forefathers fought the slave traders, killing their "masters" before being killed themselves.

After one to six months of hell on sea, depending on the waves, the sea sickness, and the destination, the slaves had the "privilege" of getting off on land in chains and cages, only to be made a spectacle of on the auction blocks. They were bartered away like beasts—mothers going to one state, fathers to another, and children to yet other locations. Just think of the pain the African mothers had to endure, their children stolen away from their grasps and gone forever. It is necessary at this point to define "master"—a misnomer as regards the slave owner. There are nice meanings of the word *master*, but not as it is used in slavery and dehumanization. The slave owner was a sadist. He derived his technique from the Marquis de Sade—that is, he takes pleasure in inflicting torturous pain on his victims. This definition is completely in line with the slave owner; his objective is not only to get his work done for free, but also to enjoy his sadistic pleasures simultaneously. Just imagine leaving Africa only to be literally owned by the sadist, moved from state to state, having to cope with the new environments like winter, without shoes and proper clothing, sleeping on floors in cold barns, coping with new languages and hideous barbarisms.

In the new environment, there were new rules or laws—no history, language, or culture to be mentioned save that of work and the whip from A.M. to when master said it was P.M. The following are some of the penalties meted out for "crimes":

praying—ten lashes; speaking African—tied to the stake, whipped and brined; trying to read or even look at a book—loss of one eye or castration; attempting to escape—split in half by being tied to two horses simultaneously running in opposite directions, being eaten by dogs trained in the art of disembowelment, or being buried shoulder deep in sand with molasses placed on the head and then torturously eaten alive by mad ants. Slaves were required to wear tags like licensed dogs. These are some of the *smaller* penalties that the Africans had to pay for fighting the horror of slavery. Do not weep or despair; I promised to tell it like it was. Breeding farms were places where mothers and sons, fathers and daughters were forced into fornication to produce a strong beast, just like what is done today with dogs or horses. Imagine the horrors our great great-grandmothers and grandfathers experienced living through more than six hundred years of hell. They ate garbage for survival, slept in pig pens, and were used for sexual pleasures. They were indoctrinated to spy on their brothers and sisters, always keeping the master sadist informed. I have mentioned only some of the things that were done to mankind by man, and that's why I said there are no words that can *really* describe slavery. Present terminology referring to slavery conveys only a fraction of the hells that Blacks went through and are going through in many areas of the world.

DEHUMANIZATION OF AFRICA'S CHILDREN

At this point, I would like to mention the dehumanization process. When millions of humans were stolen from Africa, they were stolen from flourishing civilizations. As history books and artifacts show, Africans had built previous empires and were then participants of empire building—they were Africans from Ghana, Mali, Nigeria, Morocco, Ethiopia, or any of the other states. After being captured and placed on slave ships and transported against their will to various places in Europe, the Americas, and the West Indies, they became *negroes*—a carefully planned scheme. As we all should know, this new and demeaning identity was the start of the process of dehumanization. You can read more of this in the book *The Name Negro and Its Origin and Evil Use*, written by the able historian Richard B. Moore. I recommend that you read this book, which is a classic. At this stage, the African parents became negroes and negresses —male and female animals. They were then put through a process of denial by threats, intimidation, and brute force, so that after two generations they became demoralized and disoriented in regard to their history, culture, language, and knowledge of self. That many submitted to the new life of the negro and negress created for our grandparents everything and anything except our rightful identity as Africans. A nigger or negro worked for the master whenever the master said so, and the master *always* said so. They did work like beasts for the master after the dehumanization process, somewhat like an animal would respond to orders after being trained, except the good house nigger whom master kept around the house. This slave sat under the table while his master ate; he was fed crumbs and bones like a dog, and he licked his master's toes and was used for various pleasures. The villainous field nigger kept the master-sadist informed of all the moves of the other field workers, after having gained their confidence. This is a minor description of a nigger. I repeat here, do not weep or despair but absorb this knowledge, for I am just telling it like it was and still is. The great great-grandmothers and grandfathers of Africa's children were used for sexual pleasures, used for developing special strains of strong workers, and used for breeding as if they were horses or pigs. After dozens of years of hell called civilization, some of their minds were destroyed—they were warped and mixed up. The proud Africans became personal property and were no longer thought of as what they truly were and are, *Africans*.

The most hideous act done in the process of dehumanization was the slave masters' attempt to take the genius out of the Africans. With due respect to the slaves and what they endured to survive, much success was achieved by the slave masters in this endeavor—this intelligence "deprogramming." The history of rebellion against this so-called system of civilization is documented all over the world, namely in North and South America, Africa, Europe, China, India, and the West Indies—and the struggle for equality is still going on. I repeat here, just so that there is no misunderstanding, that during the hundreds of years of dehumanization, Africans did not all submit. Some of the familiar names of rebellion are: Harriet Tubman, Nat Turner, Jomo Kenyata, Martin Luther King, Jr., Malcolm X, Patrice Lumumba, Agostino Neto, Marcus Garvey, Denmark Vesey, Cyril Murray, Kwame Nkrumah, Sojourner Truth and Gamal Nasser. These rebels are among many hundreds, all in their own way rejecting the system of chains.

Now use your mind's eye to try and assess the scenes of over six hundred years of hell, keeping in mind that what I have mentioned is only a fraction of what the horrors were like; but despite the horrendous trauma, many Blacks survived and were able to stay sane and contribute to civilization, bringing forth inventions and creations when it was all but impossible for them to do so. No slavery had any comparison to that slavery perpetrated by the Europeans against Africa's children. With deep sadness I write like it was and still is. The system of inequality still obtains—the means may have changed but the aim is still the same. The progress of the world has advanced, first with the stolen legacy of Black history and technology and then with free labor and the trade of African bodies. Yes! Exchanged or bartered for rum, molasses, sugar, tobacco, and dollars. Do not get the idea that I am referring to the United States alone, but also England, France, Portugal, Spain, Australia, Belgium, and Germany, to name some. I am sure you can add others.

Pleasures of this horrendous crime, for example, are still being perpetrated by the Dutch in Monomotapa, alias the Union of South Africa, and Zimbabwe, alias Rhodesia. The master-sadist is continuing to enjoy his pleasures using all types of tactics and defenses in these areas. He is still arguing and trying to prove that he owns and belongs to the area without the pigment—the stamp of identity—which is so necessary in the justification. He is still trying to fool us into believing that he is truly African. It is difficult to imagine that some of the Black fore-fathers were still able to stay sane after having gone through several hundred years of slavery. Reflect here a bit, use the mind's eye—they remained sane enough to continue and survive, so that millions of Blacks are here today. What is it that enabled them to survive, and why did they not give up and die? It *can* be put in a nutshell—it was the genius of being African that kept them alive. This is what I mean when I emphasize and repeat and repeat DO NOT ever fall asleep again. Historians report tens of millions of Africans died in the process of the horrendous crime of slavery. This is what mankind did to man. The slave traders tried to prove and even legally decreed that the Black forefathers were not men. This is history, too—Black history. It is the sad part of it, but it is history, and therefore I could not step over it. Untold millions of Africans died as a result, not just in North America, but all over.

Again, I must state that slavery was not accepted by the imprisoned, as some historians have tried to document. Slaves fought on the piers, on the boats, the slave blocks, and in the fields for liberation, for manhood; but they were subdued time and time again. They never gave up, however, and today Blacks are still fighting for their rights in North and South America, the Caribbean, and Africa. I say this to point out that subjuga-tion was not accepted or welcomed by the Africans.

Yes, the Africans' genius was silenced, and they were still able—under mental and physical toil, degradation, dehumaniza-tion and deprivation—to aspire and to achieve what they did. It is time for Africa's children to wake up to their genius—they don't need intoxicants to wake them up. They did not need intoxicants to persevere, communicate, and store their history and culture in their minds until they could release their knowl-edge. I leave you to tell me why Blacks need intoxicants to wake up. Intoxicants damage the mind's eye and put the Black genius asleep, and in time kill it.

There are no people on earth who have contributed to the

world as Africans have. Africa's children gave the world CIVILIZA-
TION and all it entails. So the call to Africa's children is *wake up
genius, pick up where you left off, and continue despite all the
pressures, drawbacks, and setbacks; continue like the forefathers
to show who is* MAN; *your work is cut out for you in the remain-
ing chapters, and I hope, if for no other reason but appreciation
and reverence of your grandparents' endurance, you will persevere.*

7

From Here to Eternity

The current generation does not ask who Malcolm X, Martin Luther King, Jr., or Stokeley Carmichael was. These names are known—they are synonymous with rebellion and civil rights protests; in short, they are familiar to most people. But mention names like Granville T. Woods, Marcus Garvey or Dr. Daniel Hale Williams and you would be asked these questions: Who is Granville T. Woods? Who is Marcus Garvey? Who is Daniel Hale Williams?

The point I am making here is this—things that happen are remembered for a period of months, or years, depending on their significance or importance at the time, also by their political clout and/or by their economic measure. When Dr. King started the protest movement, it was very religious in nature; the Bible was quoted, and "turn your other cheek" was the criterion for action that went on for some time. Hundreds got hurt and put in jail, and some were whipped and killed; fire hoses, cattle prods, attack dogs, torches from the brave KKK and such religious orders, and other weapons were used to terrorize peaceful demonstrations against the master. However, when the protests started having economic clout—such as closing down factories and bus lines—they then made headlines in the papers, magazines, and television, showing the loss of revenue, property and so forth. Malcolm X made his headlines, among other things, by calling whites "the devils," and proving his point by refusing to go along with turning the other cheek. Instead, his biblical guide was "an eye for an eye and a tooth for a tooth." Stokeley Carmichael made his headlines by calling the white man a name, "honkey," and by pointing out the value of the match against the military and industrial complex.

You might at this point be saying, "Where is the writer coming from now?" The point here is that these men were making their contributions within grasp of recent memory—the time factor makes it easy to remember. They are very important and necessary Africans, and we will readily attend a function or parade for either one. So too are there many very necessary Africans with whom Blacks are not currently familiar, but to whom they should pay as much, and in some instances more, homage as they presently pay contemporary leaders. If only Blacks knew of these people.

As was previously asked, who was Granville T. Woods? He was a great inventor (1856-1910) who patented over one hundred electrical and mechanical inventions. Marcus Garvey (1887-1940) was the seeker and the teacher of Africans and African redemption. He kept Africa alive for Africa's children—"Africa for the Africans at home and abroad"—and passed the flame onto Blacks of succeeding generations. In 1919, he was waving the flag of pride and dignity with his community development ideas of social and economic togetherness. Making Blacks feel proud was one of his chief interests. Dr. Daniel Hale Williams (1856-1931) did the world's first heart surgery—he was a pioneer of this specialty. The difference between these three African brothers and Malcolm X and Martin Luther King, Jr., is that the former made their contributions much before the latter, and these achievements are not common knowledge today. However, they are *all* very valuable to the system, as they have kept civilization moving in a most progressive way.

It was not so long ago that a great scientist said that the Black people excelled in sports because that endeavor does not require much intelligence, a commodity that Africans are very short of. I am not as informed on sports as much as others are, but I shall discuss this later on. I know the African fathers contributed music—did they excel in that area because it required very little intelligence? I know the Africans contributed the art of writing and drawing—did that, too, require very little intelligence? Blacks were the greatest scientists, doctors, and engineers; they laid the groundwork and built civilizations. I suppose that did not require much intelligence. While in captivity, dehumanized, and with a minimum of education, slaves were able to make contributions. The African George Washington Carver (1864-1943) saved the South with his scientific knowledge. He discovered hundreds of valuable products from the soybean and peanuts and discovered various soil fertilizers. If he did all these things with a minimum of effort and intelligence, could you imagine his contribution if he had a full brain!

Take a look at the Sphinx, located in Africa, in Egypt to be specific; it has been sitting there thousands of years—a colossus 194 feet long and 66 feet high—as Black and beautiful as ever. Present-day scientists are trying to figure out how the forefathers built this and many other works of art and their significance in pre-history. Are scientists in the dark about this knowledge, or are they just silent? Hundreds of documents and scrolls have been discovered over the years. From them the discoverers learned the African art of writing, painting, medicine, law, religion, and so forth. In other words, the Africans left the information of all their contributions. Is it not strange, though, that they did not leave any information on their technology? Use your mind's eye.

It has been theorized that the Sphinx, the statues on Easter Island and Central America, Laventa Man in South America, and many other monuments were deposited at the various locations by some unknown force or spacemen, and that these men were white. Again, this is another attempt to discredit the Black forefathers. Use your mind's eye here too. Just imagine white men coming from outer space and leaving images such as the Sphinx and Laventa Man (see *National Geographic*, February 1947, p. 160, plates IX and XVI). These white men allegedly came and left gigantic African images, wearing space helmets. Ask yourself why these white spacemen did not leave white, Indian, or Chinese images? If spacemen delivered these gigantic works of science, then the spacemen were Black, just like the images they left. Would you not say this?

If I sound like I am drifting, it is because I am traveling back in time to show how significant these things were and are. The more distant an event is in time, the less we are concerned, and the less information we have, the less interest. These few facts are very important; for example, if someone today discovered gold, bronze, copper, iron, or some other valuable substance, there would be a whole history of comment, background, and fame would be rightfully attached to the discoverers. These contributions were made by the African fathers, and there is need to praise them. Since we do not have their names, we praise Africa and Africans for their contributions. Why is so much time, money, and energy devoted to attempts to sell Africa and her children short. The white population associates the Africans' skin pigment with inferiority; paradoxically, the whites seek this pigment by following the sun. The whites even consider the African brain to be inferior. Why isn't more time and money spent on African education facilities? With their "inferior" brains, Africa's children could never be a threat, so they should be allowed to go to school as much as they like, would you not say?

Hundreds of years have been spent attempting to blot out Black history, to change it around, to make it seem as if Blacks were all slaves, that they never had direction or ambition, and hence could not make a contribution. This attempt was so well done that it left Africans ashamed of their ancestors and of themselves. (When I say Africans I mean those on the continent and those abroad.) Ask yourself why, and then use your mind's eye. I said earlier in the book that I would be repetitious, and I know I am especially so now with the mind's eye; but by this point in time, I am sure you agree with me on the need for repetition.

The Black forefathers did not leave a sufficient number of documents to prove all their contributions, but the dates, places, and images of the artifacts make these items proof of their contributions. There were always a sufficient number of Africans present to pass on the information of their history—this is why we are grateful to men of the nineteenth and twentieth centuries like George Padmore, Marcus Garvey, W. E. B. Du Bois, John Hendrik Clark, Cyril T. Murray, Elijah Muhammed, Malcolm X, Frederick Douglass, J. A. Rogers, and Richard Moore, to name just a few, for keeping the history and knowledge of Black perseverance alive. Because these men have kept this information flowing, Blacks have come along as they did, but not as much as they were able to—and they will not fully develop until they *all* become more involved in the history of their fathers, which is the key to their locked-up brains.

A greater number of Africa's children would be encouraged or motivated to study medicine if their fathers, mothers, or close relatives were in the field; such a proposition can easily be extended to engineering, law, or any of the other sciences, skills, and trades. All these things can be done as soon as Africa's children get back to using the most amazing computer, the brain, which has information locked within. When you have completed reading this book, read it again; then get ready to search and find out where your contribution to civilization lies. Do not be led to believe that you can contribute only if you have been to school, because this is not true. Many discoveries and inventions have been made by people who have had a minimum of book learning, such as the Blacks during slavery; on the other hand, do not use this as an excuse not to get education. The more informed one is, the better the chance of contributing to one's life, family, and nation.

I previously mentioned that I was not very informed on sports; this does not prevent me, however, from mentioning a few champions of African descent: soccer—Pele, the greatest player the world has ever seen; tennis—Arthur Ashe and Althea Gibson; boxing—Joe Louis, Muhammad Ali, and Sugar Ray Robinson; cricket—Gary Sobers and Lerrie Constantine; baseball —Jackie Robinson, Roy Campanella, Willie Mays, and Hank Aaron. There is not enough space to mention all the Black sports stars. I've just mentioned a few African athletes that I am aware of, and each and every one has been a superstar in his field. I remember when Jackie Robinson started playing professional ball; he just about revolutionized that business and made many people rich as a result. Stars like Willie Mays and Hank Aaron continued to enrich that business. So, too, did it happen with Pele, Muhammad Ali, Joe Louis, and many others. How about the basketball stars and track stars? As a result of their skills and talents, hundreds of millions of dollars have been contributed to the business. As I think of it right now, remove Blacks from the sports and music industry and these industries will just about die. The planners of the current civilization, I am sure, have figured out all these things for economic reasons— I am speaking of sports entertainment, the music industry, theater, and movies—but apart from their monetary rewards, there are social and cultural benefits. As previously stated, the system would stagnate without these so very necessary contributions. What I have tried to develop in this chapter is the relationship of all African brothers to each other and to mankind —particularly their continuous contributions to civilizaiton. The Sphinx, Laventa Man, Marcus Garvey, and Martin Luther King, Jr., all represent Africa and Africans.

THE TIME CLOCK

To give you an idea how long brother Sphinx has been sitting out in the African desert, I will use this type of gauge. Bear with me and try to understand my purpose and reasoning.

A.D. 1969—Africans are still enslaved in Rhodesia, South Africa, Angola, Mozambique, and Southwest Africa.

1961—President Patrice Lumumba is assassinated in the Congo.

1939—Second World War begins.

1914—First World War begins.

1898—Paul Robeson is born. He would become an accomplished actor, singer, and athlete.

1874—Arthur Schomberg, an African from Puerto Rico, is born. He would become a great writer, and a library in Harlem would eventually bear his name.

1861—My great grandmother is born. She would later relate a great deal of historical information to me.

1784—Chaka unifies the Zulu Empire in South Africa and a great military strategist.

1619—Africans are brought to North America as slaves.

1600—The mighty Songhay Empire is flourishing in Africa.

1100—The Empire of Mali is in bloom.

400—The rise of the great Empire of Ghana.

Christ is born in accord with the religious scriptures, and this we know is very far back.

B.C. 660—An Ethiopian, General Taharka becomes a Pharoah in Egypt.

700—Sabacon, an Ethiopian, rules Egypt.

720—A Nubian King, Piankhi, conquers Egypt.

900—Makeda Balkis, the Queen of Sheba, rules Ethiopia.

1350—King Tutankhamen rules Egypt.

1360—King Akhenaton (Tutankhamen's father) rules Egypt.

You can keep drifting back further and further by my gauge of time, because there are many others who are very significant. So that my list does not become boring, I will use a short cut in years, and one day in the future you and I can fill in some of the gaps in time.

2450—King Mycerinus builds the third pyramid.

2500—King Chefren builds the second pyramid.

2600—King Khufu rules Egypt.

2980—Iuem-Hotep is living; he is the father of chemistry, medicine, and music, among other things.

3000—Prince Ra Hotep is living; he is believed to be the son of King Menes.

3100—King Menes rules Egypt.

4162—King Amen-Ra rules Nubia, Ethiopia, Egypt, Arabia, and Persia; his subjects at the time are all Black.

4478—King Ori is ruling Ethiopia.

4500—An African, described as a bushman-type Black, founds the first dynasty in Egypt.

This is my time clock, used merely as a gauge in time to see how far back the African fathers have stamped their identity on this earth, so that no one, NO ONE, will mistake their identity.

Electricity for common use was developed in the nineteenth century. The world was greatly enhanced by this discovery, but as important as electricity is, all the essentials of civilization presupposed its advent. In other words, light and power were generated by other sources of energy. The old lamplighter traveled his route as late as 1923 and lit the lamps at night. The houses were lit by candles and kerosene lamps. There were no radios, TV, or electrical appliances, no computers, calculators, or other electronic devices. The point I am making is that all of the necessities or qualifications for a civilization were already there—civilization just received an electrical shot in the arm! No one man is credited with this shot in the arm, and although electricity was known about 2500 years ago, it took years for it to be utilized into the energy we now use. Granville T. Woods, known as one of the world's greatest electricians, is a great part of this foundation with his dozens of electrical contributions. So is F. M. Jones. I do not intend to distort this contribution or any other, but I am making sure that Africa's children get the glory they deserve.

I am trying to show the attack by learned men on the African brain—measuring it and constantly attacking its ability to compete with the European brain. These "scholars" have spent much time and untold millions of dollars trying to manufacture proof of the big lie, while at the same time showing fear of competition by denying, wherever possible, even by force, the opportunity for Africa's children to attend the halls of learning. This is no secret indeed—it is common knowledge all over the world.

THE STEEL BAND

In the late thirties, Africans living in Trinidad contributed a series of instruments that later came to be known as the steel band. The contribution, modified several times since then, has become known as one of the greatest contributions to music in the twentieth century, thanks to men like Spree Simon, Neville Jules, Eli Manet, Oscar Pile, and many others.

If you have not had the opportunity to look at and listen to a steel band in operataion, you should; then draw your conclusions about the contribution of an entire musical orchestra in the twentieth century by Africa's children in Trinidad, the likes of which are not known in this world. Many accomplished musicians are amazed at the ability of these musicians to copy any musical arrangement, whether they can read music or not. I have just briefly touched on another African contribution to civilization, which we take for granted. Use your mind's eye to fully see this great contribution.

Just remember some of the hells and tortures the Black foreparents went through, and note that Blacks are still here—so keep the flag waving. Don't despair, get out and make your contribution in whatever your field or endeavor may be. Don't forget that Africa's children have a contribution to make and can do so once their mind's eye is awakened; prepare not to let the mind's eye be clouded again and always be ready to defend the mind's eye. It's certain at this stage that you are aware of what you have to do to protect and preserve it. No one else can be the doctor of your mind's eye; you have and know the prescription to keep it healthy. Just use it. There is no excuse. The world awaits your contribution, however simple or small.

Summary

Much has been said in the previous chapters, and hence much will be challenged and doubted. There will be many upsets as a result, both pleasant and shocking to many people. I tried to keep the history as simple as possible to make all readers find it easy to read and informative. I hope I have accomplished what I promised, for as stated, the study of history does become boring. Africa's history, though, is the world's way of life, unlike any other history, and without knowledge of it, Black pride, dignity, and the ability to compete is *controlled*.

In summary, from the beginning God created this universe and placed man in it, with other forms of life at his disposal. We must assume that God chose to make man the higher form of life that he is. God left man in the cradle in the heart of Africa, and from this we can assume that the first man was Black. Being merciful, God left us with all the necessities for survival. From this location, the Black foreparents lived and multiplied, and in the course of time moved South of Tanzania and spread to the North, East, and West.

The Africans developed various cultures along the way, leaving trails of clues to their identity as they traveled—for example, the works seen in all Black African cultures. The iron cultures came from the area of Zimbabwe, gold and bronze from Ethiopia and Ghana. As the anthropologists and archeologists continue to assess the scene, more cultures will be discovered in Southern Africa, for here is where it all began. In and through these various cultures, many civilizations were developed. We analyzed what the world would be like if we removed some of the greatest contributions of the African fathers, such as gold and silver, paper, pens, ink and paint, also wood, iron, brick and stone, the sciences of chemistry, medicine, astronomy, agriculture, and the arts of music, painting, and theater. Yes, these were all contributions of Africa's children. We tried to visualize the state of the world without their contributions, and saw a great wilderness. We observed and traveled hundreds of years up and down and across Africa's great highways by way of the mind's eye. We watched all the developments of man and evaluated his accomplishments.

I spoke of Africa's children—not only on the African continent but all over the world. I tried to show how many Europeans have tried and continue to try to adopt Africa's name and identity, and we decided that it could never be allowed. I pointed out many African contributions—for example, musical instruments, the arts of dancing, acting, and singing, which, among other things, entertain and tranquilize the world. Try to think of the world without music! Africans also contributed religion, the most profound element of civilization.

I have shown how the contents of the world have not changed that much—how the fundamentals are the cornerstones of progress. Man still lives in houses similar to those existing thousands of years ago. The contents, such as tables, chairs, and beds, are the same now as then; there are modifications in design, of course, but not that much. Interior decorations, such as vases, pottery, and knick-knacks, are still the same. Ancient African jewelry, which is breathtaking and intricately beautiful, rivals the finest works of art today. Personal decorations, such as cosmetics and trinkets, have hardly changed. There was the development of agriculture—tilling the soil, planting, harvesting, and storing the food. The domestication and raising of livestock was another original contribution to the development of civilization.

I mentioned the discovery of hundreds of scrolls and the wealth of information therein. These scrolls contain many lessons for the world, but many people today, particularly Blacks, have no knowledge of this, since the contents were not all made public.

Developing the time clock was my way of showing how long Africa's children have been vital movers of civilization. The time clock was my way of giving as much information as possible, while trying not to bore the reader with many details.

Can you imagine the wealth of knowledge that is missing concerning the great Black contributions? This is where your part comes into play in completing this book. There are many years of the time clock to be checked and filled in. For example, if you are interested in medicine, you might like to know how it all came about. You are aware that you cannot know by just what you hear or have been told, so the next logical step is to do some searching on your own. In the process you must now go to the libraries and museums to read and observe. In this process, you arrive at the fact that Hippocrates is the father of medicine. Since this is the information that is available, you accept this and say, "This is where it began, in Greece." Sometime after in your discussion on this subject, you begin to doubt this, and you are forced to go back and research. Upon further investigation, you find out that medicine was being practiced in Africa 4500 years ago, and that medicine was specialized at that time, and your intelligence would let you know that if Africans were specializing at that date, they would have had a few hundred years of experience prior to the time of specialties. You would now have to keep on searching to find out the specialties, and how these African doctors diagnosed ailments and prescribed treatments. In so doing, you would be led to the beginning. You can use the same process here to trace all the skills, trades, arts, and professions to these original contributors. There is so much to be traced back to the great forefathers, and it is my hope that many will be motivated to come forward and contribute their genius.

I would like to see a theological student do a thorough study of religion back to its base, gather up all the ancient information on the matter, and present a systematic report. This can also be done, as I mentioned before, with the sciences.

As I continue to review and summarize, I hope your mind's eye—unclouded by intoxicants and poisons that damage the brain in which you have the wisdom of the forefathers locked in—is used all the time. From this day on never do anything or allow anyone to influence you to do anything that would jeopardize the flow of knowledge. The flow of knowledge that I refer to is your contribution, however small it may seem; as previously stated, do not get the idea that you cannot contribute without first receiving higher education, because this is not true. The fact is the contributions are locked up in the brain and need the environment to come forth.

In discussing slavery, I tried to expose it for what it really was, as sad and humiliating as it was. The hundreds of hells slavery represented to Africa's children exists right now in South America and South Africa, among other places, where Blacks work for the master-sadist for little pay and unending hours, restricted from use of various facilities and places, and treated and housed like cattle. But despite all the trauma and horror of dislodging the information from the African mind, many Blacks were able to stay sane and pass on some of the wisdom of the forefathers, so that even during the period of slavery, Blacks made significant contributions.

I wish I could have avoided the discussion of slavery, the dehumanization process, and the designs of the master—but I promised to tell it like it was and still is, despite the painful horrors that these years brought to Africa's children. Africa's children should not be silent on the price their foreparents paid in blood and sweat. We are constantly reminded of the sufferings of various nationalities via the communication media, and much time and money is spent against the enemies of the people in their struggles, and rightly so; but the rape of Africa and her children continues in an intolerable nonchalant manner, as though it does not matter. Really, it does not matter unless the people who feel the pain and terror start shouting out about it at every opportunity, hour by hour, day by day.

One hundred million human beings were destroyed by the masters of deception, torture, greed, and terror in every way imaginable. No section of human society has such a high death toll to bear as Africans, as a result of man's inhumanity to mankind. That a slave child during many years of torture and dehumanization could still make scientific contributions disposes one to ask the profound question—How much more could have been achieved had Blacks been actively encouraged to contribute? To use a current quotation, "A mind is a terrible thing to waste."

We have used the mind's eye to primarily look into the past. In that glorious past, we have become acquainted with the genius of Africa's children. Here are just a few of the greatest contributors and their contributions:

The elevator—A. Miles
The air-conditioning unit—F. M. Jones
The light bulb carbon filament—Lewis Latimer
The lawn mower—F. Burr
The electric railway trolley—E. R. Robinson
The subway third rail, railway telegraphy—Granville T. Woods
The traffic signal—Garrett Morgan

As I look to the future with my mind's eye, I see millions of people who are alert and who are making contributions for the good of mankind.

Even though I am not a learned historian, I probably could have written a book explaining each historical event and discovery in detail; but my intention was not to bore my readers with many details. We agreed that the history of hundreds of thousands of years could not all be told in such a short time—your reason, then, for continuing to read on is to liberate your mind's eye, which holds the secrets of your contributions. I do hope that you are motivated and, as a result, interested to the extent that you will continue to delve into the histories of the African forefathers, for what I have mentioned only outlines their incredible contributions.

I can think of no other way to end this book than with the following statement. It is not what Africa and her children contributed to the world, but rather *what didn't* they contribute to the world—for Africa's children have given the world civilization. Again, I must repeat for the last time, USE YOUR MIND'S EYE!